ANYTHING IS POSSIBLE WITH BALLET

STEVEN McRAE
illustrated by Margaux Carpentier

Magic Cat Publishing

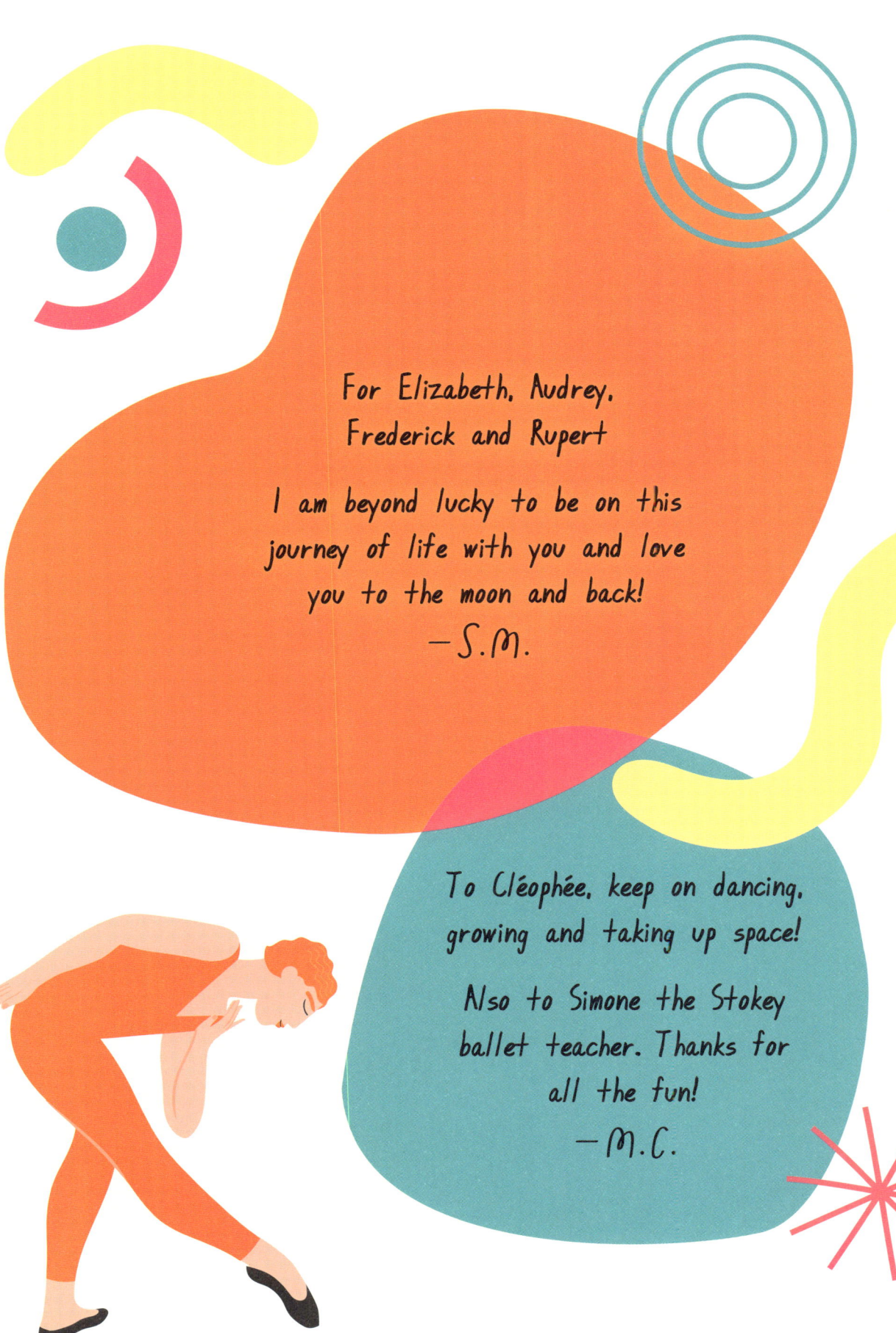

For Elizabeth, Audrey, Frederick and Rupert

I am beyond lucky to be on this journey of life with you and love you to the moon and back!
—S.M.

To Cléophée, keep on dancing, growing and taking up space!

Also to Simone the Stokey ballet teacher. Thanks for all the fun!
—M.C.

CONTENTS

4-5	INTRODUCTION
6-7	DANCE IS A LANGUAGE!
8-9	PREPARATION
10-11	LISTEN TO YOUR BODY
12-13	SELF-CARE
14-15	IN THE STUDIO
16-17	BASIC POSITIONS
18-19	LEGS
20-21	FEET
22-23	ARMS
24-25	PORT DE BRAS
26-27	CORE
28-29	EYES
30-31	EXTENSIONS
32-33	MOVING
34-35	BARREWORK
36-39	FOUNDATIONAL MOVES
40-43	JUMPS
44-45	POINTE WORK
46-47	PAS DE DEUX
48-49	RÉVERÉNCE
50-51	IN REHEARSAL
52-55	PREPARING FOR A PRODUCTION
56-57	NEW WORKS
58-59	MUSIC
60-61	TRANSFERRING TO THE STAGE
62-63	BEHIND THE SCENES
64-65	THE TEAM
66-67	NERVES
68-69	EXPLODE ONTO THE STAGE
70-71	GLOSSARY

MY NAME IS STEVEN McRAE

I am a father, husband and dancer with one of the world's greatest ballet companies, the Royal Ballet in London.

I grew up in a motorsport family in Sydney, Australia, miles away from any theatres. But at the age of seven, after watching my sister dancing, I asked to attend a class.

I can remember that first lesson: my teacher ignited a passion within me that has since taken me all over the world.

At the age of seventeen, I won a scholarship at an international ballet competition in Switzerland that enabled me to train for a year at the Royal Ballet School in London. A year later, I was offered a job with the Royal Ballet Company. Today, I am a principal dancer with the company and I get to perform all over the world with some of the greatest artists of a generation.

Dance quite literally opened the world up to me. I have discovered so much about who I am, what I am passionate about, how to overcome obstacles and what it is like to pursue a dream — even when no one else believes in it.

I have experienced the highs of this powerful art form, performing on the world's greatest stages. I have also experienced extreme lows: snapping my Achilles tendon live on stage at the Royal Opera House nearly brought my career to an end. However, what the world of dance has taught me is that anything is possible if you have a passion, an indomitable will and the ability to open yourself up to the extraordinary world we live in.

DANCE IS A LANGUAGE!

I can perform anywhere in the world and, without speaking a word, I get to have a conversation with the audience and share a unique moment in time with them.

Ballet should be seen as a language that can be used to communicate in ways that words sometimes cannot. In this book, you may come across terms that sound intimidating, or perhaps you recognize them by different names.

But remember, there are no real rules in dance, so take the information shared in this book and go and create your own unique way of moving.

This book is for everyone — ballet is for everyone — and ballet can provide the foundation blocks that many other dance styles build upon.

Just as an alphabet provides the framework for different languages, so too do the core basics of ballet provide all dancers with the foundations to one day fly!

INTRODUCTION

Express yourself through dance, and ultimately you will have a new way of communicating with the world.

PREPARATION

Dancers need to respect their bodies, just like athletes. Warming up is a very personal activity and dancers are becoming more and more guided by sports science to understand how they can best prepare their bodies for the daily demands of dancing.

WARMING UP

To genuinely express yourself as a dancer you need your body to have total freedom, and so it is essential to warm up first.

You can warm up in lots of ways, such as doing floor and gym exercises, Pilates or even cycling.

Developing core strength is essential

INTRODUCTION

FUEL

A dancer's body is like a supercar. If you put rubbish fuel into a supercar, it simply won't function to the best of its capabilities and you could even damage it. Your body is exactly the same: safely fuelling and caring for the instrument that is the human body is an essential part of your preparation.

HEART RATE

Raising your heart rate and allowing blood to flow around your body through active movement, rather than traditional static stretching, will safely prepare you for class.

MUSIC

Music can have a powerful effect on us, so it is no surprise that many dancers include music in their warm-up routines.

Strengthen your feet and ankles

LISTEN TO YOUR BODY

When you are able to assess your own body, you can inform others of any concerns you have.

NOTICE

Being aware of any areas of tightness, pain or restriction in your body will help guide you and your teachers, coaches and choreographers to make smart decisions during your class or rehearsal.

Navigating injuries requires mental and physical support

INTRODUCTION

FOCUS

Taking care of your mental wellbeing is also incredibly important as our mental and physical wellbeing are connected to each other.

Find a quiet spot, then close your eyes and breathe slowly from your belly.

LISTEN TO YOUR MIND

SELF-CARE

If you choose to dance more regularly — especially if you want to pursue dance as a career — you must learn how to properly take care of yourself, both mentally and physically.

Sometimes part of self-care involves taking a step back — or even a break — so that you can fully appreciate just how much passion you have for dance.

DO NOTHING!

READ & WRITE

INTRODUCTION

CREATE

More doesn't always equal more

Your passion for exploring the extraordinary art form of ballet is essential to your development as a young dancer.

When you are passionate about something, it can be tricky to juggle academic work and other hobbies, and find time for family and friends, as well as YOU, the individual.

It can be difficult to accept that more doesn't always equal more. But it's an important lesson to learn.

Fuelling yourself with good nutrition, taking time away from dance to recover (if needed, with a programme guided by science) — as well as learning to prioritize your workload will all add up to a happier, healthier you.

GET OUTSIDE

TAKE A BREAK

BASIC POSITIONS

Ballet helps you build a strong foundation and technique, whatever your style of dance. These five basic positions are the core shapes of ballet, and all ballet dancers — from beginners to professionals — use them at the beginning and end of a movement.

SECOND POSITION

Arms wide like wings

Fingers soft

Elbows up

Feet apart, toes facing outwards

FIRST POSITION

Arms in an oval shape

Fingers curved, index (pointer) finger extended

Turnout movements come from the hip

Toes pointing outwards

LEGS

Imagine your legs to be engines launching a rocket to the moon! They can power you off the floor, support you — and anyone you may be holding up — and help you change direction. They also provide you with the stability you need to create moments of stillness, speed and strength.

ALIGNMENT

By learning all the ways you can move your legs, you'll understand how to safely navigate the challenges of dance. Working on correct alignment is not only useful for visual communication but it is also crucial for protecting the bones, muscles, joints, tendons and ligaments in your body.

What goes up...

IN THE STUDIO

Did you know that several times your body weight goes through your joints when you land from a big jump?

Your legs provide you with the power to leave the ground... and shock absorbers to safely return to the ground.

...must come down!

FEET

Your feet, just like your eyes and hands, can help you to tell a story and convey an emotion. They also provide you with a platform that you can construct your 'building' on.

DEMI POINTE

FOUNDATION

Did you know that there are 26 bones, 33 joints, 19 muscles, dozens of tendons and hundreds of ligaments in each of your feet? All of these intertwine, providing you with little engines at the ends of your legs!

IN THE STUDIO

FROM THE FLOOR UP

When you dance, you use your entire being to express yourself. So, try to think about your feet – as well as your hands, head and everything else – as an extension of your body.

Fly through the air with your entire being

10 FINGERS AND 10 TOES

Hands and feet have different structures, but they also have many similarities. Try to visualize using your feet to express yourself in the same way that you use your hands.

Pianists have an incredible ability to isolate and use each of their fingers to control the sounds they make when they hit the piano keys. As a dancer, you too can think of your hands and feet as a tool that will help you 'play' the instrument that is your body.

ARMS

Ask most people what they think ballet looks like and they will probably lift their arms high above their head and start spinning. Learning basic ballet arm positions is the next part of the journey towards expressing yourself through dance.

FOURTH POSITION

To start with, you'll learn the port de bras — the five basic arm positions — but over time you'll understand how to move your arms in a way that they become extensions of your whole body.

Think of the arms reacting like a wave...

IN THE STUDIO

EXPLORE

Different schools of training in different parts of the world will declare that there is <u>one</u> way to achieve each position that involves a specific eye level, arm height, use of epaulement (shoulder position) and so on. But the important thing to remember is to find what works for <u>you</u> and what helps you to express yourself. Dancers seek to create different shapes, movements and stories, so allow yourself to explore how your arms can communicate in various ways.

...responding to your spine and core.

PORT DE BRAS

In classical ballet, port de bras refers to the way in which you hold and move your arms. As you become more advanced, you will be taught an exercise taking you through the five basic positions. These positions will enable you to create a language with your upper body. Try to move your arms gracefully and fluidly through the different positions.

As you move your arms...

...breathe deeply to emphasize your movements.

IN THE STUDIO

BASIC HAND POSITION

Your hands are very expressive, so try not to forget about them. Shake them out and let your hands relax, then extend your middle finger and your little finger, allowing air between your fingers. Then, pull your thumb towards your index finger. Try to relieve your hands and fingers of any tension — unless you want to express something that requires sharper, spikier shapes.

Your hands should look like seamless extensions of your arms.

CORE

Freedom and abandonment is made possible through strength. Think of your body's core as your 'home base' or 'meeting point'. The more power and strength you develop over time, the more stability you will have, making your core the central power station of your body.

BALANCE

Your core includes all the muscles at the centre of your body, such as your abdominals, obliques (down the sides of your ribcage) and lower back muscles.

To have a strong core, you don't need to tense your abdominals (stomach muscles) all of the time. Rather than doing a thousand crunches every day, think about your entire body and how your core allows you to move away from your 'centre' but return back to 'home base', helping you to stabilize and control your movements.

IN THE STUDIO

Having a stable core gives you good balance, and lets you make precise, graceful movements. This is known as having 'poise'.

POISE

The more extreme your movements, the more important it is that you are able to return to a 'centred' state.

CONTROL

The more control you have, the less likely you are to injure yourself.

EYES

Dance is all about human interaction and communication. Your eyes are one of the most powerful tools you have to convey emotion. You can use them to draw an imaginary line, creating the illusion of reaching further and helping you to connect with your partner. They also help you to focus when turning, balancing and jumping.

Think of your eyes as another extension of your body

LASER VISION

To help you extend your gaze in relation to the movement of your limbs, imagine that you have lasers shooting out of your eyes that complement the line of your arms or legs. Sounds strange, but it works!

SPOTTING

Turning quickly can make you dizzy, so ballet dancers use a technique called 'spotting' to help them keep their balance as they spin.

Spotting is the number one skill to master when performing any pirouette or turn.

IN THE STUDIO

TELL A STORY

Your eyes help you to tell a story and convey emotion. Through them you can show sadness, excitement, surprise — just about every feeling! — adding depth to your performance.

Choose a spot at eye level to focus on and start to turn your body.

Twist your shoulders but keep your eyes focussed on the spot as your body turns.

Whip your head around and find your spot as you complete your turn.

EXTENSIONS

In ballet, extensions are when a dancer raises their legs in the air, either to the front, side or back. Bigger, more expansive extensions can help tell a story, provoke a reaction from the audience or paint beautiful shapes. Depending on what we are trying to say with our bodies, we might need to make ourselves as small as possible or as big as possible.

It might be tempting to push yourself into extreme positions — especially when using your legs. Don't!

When you're starting to work on your extensions, it's important to have a skilled teacher or coach to guide you. They can help you safely navigate a combination of strengthening and stretching exercises to achieve both mobility and stability. Remember, overstretching is not only dangerous but can also limit your ability to express yourself.

STORY-TELL
Never place your leg without purpose. Make it part of your narrative, whatever that may be.

BRING CONTRAST
Work within your capabilities to produce highs and lows, increased intensity and calmer moods.

MOVING

When we move to our favourite music or join in with a big group dance routine, we allow a natural freedom to take over our bodies. It's easy to forget about this freedom when the word 'ballet' is mentioned.

Ballet IS a vocabulary for your body to use while expressing yourself.

Remember: ballet is NOT a series of 'perfectly' executed positions.

My very first teacher said to me: SPIN AS <u>FAST</u> AS POSSIBLE...

IN THE STUDIO

Think of each position as a point in a dot-to-dot puzzle.

Your artistic flair joins these points together, creating a beautiful picture.

...AND JUMP AS HIGH AS YOU CAN

When you pay too much attention to the details, it is very easy to start isolating your body by focusing on your feet, or your turnout, or some other specific technical element. Try not to lose the natural freedom you felt when you first started dancing in the search for an impossible perfection.

BARREWORK

Ballet combines basic positions with basic movements. We work on these at the barre, a horizontal rail that dancers can use for support. By practising these foundational movements, you are getting ready to use and build on them when you step into the centre of the studio or onto the stage.

For instance, practising a relevé in passé at the barre prepares your body to perform a simple pirouette in the centre of the studio.

Imagine your body as a tall skyscraper

Draw your working leg up your calf

Rise onto the ball of your foot, trying to keep your balance

RELEVÉ IN PASSÉ

IN THE STUDIO

PIROUETTE

Rhythm is always your friend and this can be incredibly useful when training pirouettes or turns. Think of the number of turns you're aiming for and then follow a pulse or beat in your head to complete the turn.

Start with your arms out wide before bringing them into first position

Bring the left side of your back around

Imagine spiralling up, like a drink going up a straw

Bend your knees and push off the back leg, twisting your shoulders to the left

Complete the turn going up and then decide how to finish it

FOUNDATIONAL MOVES

These basic ballet moves are among the most adaptable: the speed and expansiveness of your movements will change what the audience feels. Different schools may try to convince you that their way is the correct way, but I truly believe that each style enables you to say something different.

DÉVELOPPÉ

A développé is where you extend your bent leg out to an open position, either in an adagio (slow) manner or at a quicker, more explosive speed. Your extended position will depend on what you would like to convey, and what is comfortable for your body to achieve.

IN THE STUDIO

ARABESQUE

An arabesque is where you stand on one leg and extend the other leg behind. The arabesque line can be used in lots of ways to convey a whole range of emotions. It can be used on its own, in pirouettes, in jumps, in supported adagio movements with a partner and even in a simple split stretch on the floor.

In Sleeping Beauty's famous Rose Adagio, Aurora stands en pointe with her leg in an attitude derrière (bent leg lifted to the back) as she is greeted by four separate princes.

The ballerinas who perform this dance are true superheroes!

CHASSÉ

This sliding movement can be used in lots of ways: to launch yourself one way or another, as a linking step, or as a finishing step at the end of a series of movements. Bending your knees can change the look of the movement, too.

ATTITUDE

An attitude movement is a slightly bent leg held in different positions. It is very common to see attitude derrière in classical ballet, especially in the *Sleeping Beauty*.

PLIÉ

Pliés act as shock absorbers for a dancer's body and can be used to slow down or speed up a movement. You can perform a plié in all five positions: bend your knees and slowly lower your body.

FONDU

A fondu is an extension of the plié, performed on one leg. It is a great way to stabilize, strengthen and support larger movements. Bend the knee of your supporting leg and slowly lower yourself. A helpful visualization for this movement is to imagine your legs pushing through sticky toffee.

ROND DE JAMBE

Literally meaning 'round of the leg', with this step you move a straightened leg in a circular movement on the floor to the side of your body. This is a good exercise for exploring how expansive you can be in your movements.

Try to trace a bigger circle with every repeated movement

RELEVÉ

Relevés are an opportunity to fire up your legs with a different intensity and to make yourself as tall as possible. Smoothly rise up onto the balls of your feet, imagining your head is trying to reach the ceiling.

EN POINTE

A relevé is one stop away from going up en pointe in pointe shoes, or leaving the floor in a jump. It takes a few years of practice before your feet will be strong enough to dance en pointe (see p44).

JUMPS

Jumps are the closest thing we humans can do to give the illusion of flying. Dancers who are able to combine coordination with strength can appear as though they are suspended in the air.

TEMPS LEVÉ

A graceful hop, starting on one foot and landing on that same foot.

PETIT ALLEGRO

Petit means little, while allegro means quick. In ballet we use this term to refer to a series of small, quick jumps, linking the five main families of jumps together.

IN THE STUDIO

SISSONNE
A jump starting on two feet and landing on a single foot.

ASSEMBLÉ
A jump starting on one leg and joining both together in the air.

Absorb each landing to protect your body, but also to give the illusion of complete ease, like a cat!

JETÉ
Any jump or giant leap from one foot to the other.

SAUTÉ
This usually means a jump in which you start and land on two feet.

BATTEMENT MOVEMENTS

To perform a battement movement, raise one leg and extend it to the front, side or back and 'beat' the air.

GRAND ALLEGRO

Grand allegro — the big jumps — are a fantastic tool for expressing yourself and the character you are portraying.

Practising a grand battement movement at the barre...

First, practise a grand battement at the barre. Hold onto the barre with two hands, then throw your working leg in the air straight from the hip, without bending your knee, and keeping your supporting leg straight.

IN THE STUDIO

BATTEMENT FONDU

Fondu means 'melting' in French, so this movement is performed very smoothly. Go slowly into plié – and then up from plié while extending your working leg out from your body.

...is the first step towards performing grand allegro centre stage.

Finally, you can replicate this movement in the centre of the studio or stage, combining the grand battement movement with a high jump, called grand allegro.

Throwing your leg high into the air helps you lift your hips higher off the floor, ultimately giving the illusion of soaring above the ground.

POINTE WORK

Pointe work is an advanced form of classical ballet, in which the dancer supports all their weight on the very tips of their toes.

DOMING

Most dancers need a full year of pre-pointe training before they are fitted with pointe shoes. You must learn to 'dome' your feet by keeping your toes flat on the ground and arching the middle of your foot into a dome shape.

ANKLE STRENGTH

Before going en pointe, your ankles, legs and core should be strong enough to support you, so that you don't injure yourself.

GOING EN POINTE

It is absolutely critical that pointe shoes are fitted by a professional, and that you start your pointe training with the guidance of a teacher or coach.

IN THE STUDIO

Pointe shoes are special ballet shoes that allow dancers to perform en pointe, giving the illusion of floating like otherworldly creatures above the floor.

FIRST IMAGINE

It can be helpful for dancers to visualize their feet behaving like hands.

Dancers work up to going en pointe by doing lots of slow, repetitive, strength-building exercises with their feet at the barre.

Professional dancers use pointe shoes to create the illusion of floating in classical ballets like *Giselle* or *Swan Lake*, but they have developed such a strong technical capability that choreographers continue to push the boundaries of what is humanly possible with the aid of the pointe shoe.

IMPORTANT

It can be dangerous to perform pointe work before the age of 12 because you could damage your growing feet.

PAS DE DEUX

In ballet, a pas de deux ('step of two') is a dance duet between two dancers. It relies on communication, connection and attentive listening between the dancers. It is crucial for the two performers to have a deep understanding of each other's movements, musical interpretation, strengths and weaknesses, along with a mutual respect for one another.

ENTRÉE

In adagio, the two dancers make slow, graceful movements together.

Entrée literally means 'entrance'. Both dancers welcome each other on stage and prepare to begin the adagio.

ADAGIO (meaning slow)

If you are supporting the other dancer in a pas de deux, it can be useful to imagine how YOU would want to feel or be placed into movements or positions if you were the one being supported.

IN THE STUDIO

SUPPORTED ADAGIO

One dancer does pointe work, while the other holds their partner close to support them.

VARIATIONS

Next, the two dancers each perform a solo, known as a variation.

CODA

Finally, the dancers come together again, ending the dance in an exciting grand crescendo, known as a coda.

RÉVERÉNCE

Ballet classes, rehearsals and performances traditionally end with a revérénce, or a simple bow or curtsy.

PROCESS THE CLASS

This moment is an opportunity to process what you have just learnt, experienced and enjoyed, and express gratitude for what you and your teachers have shared, much like performers do on stage at the end of a performance, where they share a moment of thankfulness and appreciation with the audience.

IN THE STUDIO

EXPRESS YOUR THANKS

Even as a professional dancer, I like to take a brief moment to process and acknowledge what has just taken place in a class, rehearsal or performance.

Taking the time to remember new ideas, helpful tips or constructive feedback is incredibly valuable.

This kind of reflection is best done with visualization rather than just repeating movements or steps over and over again.

Class may be over, but the practice never ends! By reliving all the moments that felt wonderful when you danced, you can continue to develop your craft while you wait to return to the studio.

PREPARING FOR A PRODUCTION

In the months running up to a production, or show, dancers enter a period of rehearsals to prepare for the performance.

LISTEN Pay attention to your director...

FOCUS ...and listen to yourself

IN REHEARSAL

BE PATIENT
Be patient with yourself and your fellow dancers as you learn.

Rehearsals allow you to test your boundaries, try new things, work through challenges and put your creativity to the test. This is where art is created.

Explore your craft, push your limits and develop the different layers of artistry you need to transport your audience to another world.

RESPOND
React to your partner

From the moment the ballet is announced and the dancers have all been cast in their parts, a dancer will ask themselves many questions...

How can I prepare my body for the physical demands of a show? Do I need any additional training to develop extra stamina, speed, mobility or strength?

What are my key challenges?

CHALLENGES

NEW WORKS

One of the greatest honours of any dancer's career is to be part of a new creation made especially for the company, school or group you are involved with. It is very rewarding to be part of something brand new and have the chance to interpret a role in a way that is totally unique to you.

The creation of new works often requires more hours than re-staging existing pieces, posing constant challenges for dancers.

Physically, this can take a toll on the body, as well as the mind, so it is even more important to monitor your wellbeing during this time.

IN REHEARSAL

The excitement of participating in a new creation comes from collaborating with fellow creatives: the other dancers, the choreographer, composers, technicians, writers, prop creators, makeup artists, lighting designers and many others.

UNIQUE TO YOU

Collectively, this team of creatives help you to create your new character, allowing you to tell a story that will hopefully transport the audience to another world and generate a new piece of living art.

MUSIC

Music and dance should work together in a partnership as one: they should support yet challenge each other, respond to each other and drive each emotionally on.

When we harness the power of music to enhance emotions, convey power or vulnerability and amplify the sheer strength of the character, the audience will bear witness to a 'tour de force'.

STANDING STILL

One of the greatest skills you can acquire as a dancer is the ability to stand still. Dancers dedicate their lives to exploring movement and freedom… but true artists are capable of remaining still too, allowing them to express a wide range of emotions to the audience.

IN REHEARSAL

THE SPIRIT OF MUSIC

Music can help to create memorable and transformative moments. When a dancer allows the music to resonate within their body, those watching can feel as though the dancer has truly *become* the music.

YOU AND THE MUSIC ARE ONE

TRANSFERRING TO THE STAGE

Rehearsals allow you to anticipate, as much as possible, what happens in a live performance. However, you can never truly replicate what it's like to be on stage in the moment: the adrenaline, excitement, nerves and expectation that come with performing LIVE in front of an auditorium full of people!

Some elements of live performance are impossible to rehearse in the studio. From performing with a live orchestra to dancing under hot stage lights in full costume and makeup, the atmosphere and energy are different every night.

Your spatial environment changes, too. Instead of facing a wall or mirrors, you suddenly confront a void between you and the other dancers on stage and the audience seated beyond the orchestra pit.

MISTAKES HAPPEN

No matter how prepared you are for this moment, it is live theatre, and we are all human. Things can, and do, go wrong.

Sometimes, changes in your environment can offer positive opportunities to develop your craft further.

Other times, it can be disorienting to adjust to bright lights, changes in the tempo of the music or even costumes that accidentally rip or snag!

Just remember that every performance is an opportunity to grow as an artist. We learn and we develop through experience!

Behind the Scenes

THE TEAM

Imagine the tip of an iceberg poking out of the ocean. This is what the audience sees when the curtain goes up and the dancer is stood centre stage. However, supporting each dancer is the rest of the iceberg hidden beneath the surface: a huge team of people working together behind the scenes.

The magic of a production relies heavily on talented artistic directors, choreographers and an orchestra, along with brilliant set and costume designers who can help turn an empty stage into a fantasy land, a historical palace, a lake, a royal court or whatever scene the story requires.

BACKSTAGE MANAGEMENT

Stage management is responsible for the safe running of every performance.

They're like backstage conductors, giving cues and instructions to all members of the technical team, from lighting to props, sound to scenery.

BEHIND THE SCENES

DANCER'S SUPPORT TEAM

Your team might include a coach, physiotherapist, psychologist, nutritionist, surgeon, shoe maker... the list goes on.

Ever wondered where the dancers' costumes come from? How do the lights magically create the beautiful atmosphere on stage? How do scene changes happen so quickly during a performance?

Every element of the performance requires a group of passionate individuals to come together as a team to make the magic happen.

NERVES

Stepping onto stage can be an exhilarating experience, and being nervous can be a good thing. But nerves can also overshadow your enjoyment. As a performer, it is important to learn to have faith in yourself and your skills, and know that whenever you go out on stage, you will always try to do your best.

The expectations that we put on ourselves should always be realistic and fair.

So much of live performance is out of your control, so take the pressure off yourself and focus on the elements you can control. Go through your warm-up and pre-performance routine, take control of the moments leading up to the curtain going up and then, after the orchestra tunes up and begins to play, embrace the beauty of performing.

BEHIND THE SCENES

TRUST YOURSELF

Self-trust is key to stepping out on stage. Only you can fully understand the work you have done to prepare for that moment. Accept that you might make mistakes. Accept that you are human. It is this human element that makes live performance so exhilarating.

Dance is an art form — it's impossible to achieve perfection, but you can strive for excellence by always trying your best.

You may just surprise yourself when you open your heart and share those magical minutes with an audience.

YOUR SUPERPOWER

Nerves are the superpower that can enable you, the artist, to open your heart to an audience. By doing this, you empower the audience to acknowledge that they, too, are human. Powerful stuff!

EXPLODE ONTO THE STAGE

There is nothing quite like flying across the stage!

As a child, in my early training, I felt like a tiger unleashed. And that is still how it feels for me when the curtain rises... even after many years of performing professionally across the world.

UNIQUE FEELING

Anticipation, excitement, fear and joy all come together, giving you a rush like no other! For that moment in time, everyone involved behind the scenes is part of something unique, but the artists on stage get to share a moment with the audience that can never again be replicated or recreated.

CONNECT

If you try to be perfect, you might leave your audience unmoved. But if you open yourself up and connect with an audience, everyone — both on and off stage — may share a transformative experience that you'll all remember forever.

MAKE MAGIC

There's a magic to live theatre that can't be replicated in film or recorded music. The audience feeds off the spontaneity and energy of a live performance, which transcends their everyday lives and allows them to dream, aspire and hold on to hope.

A TIGER UNLEASHED!

GLOSSARY

Adagio An Italian word that means 'slow'.

Arabesque A specific pose where you stand on one leg with the other lifted in the air behind you.

Assemblé A French word meaning 'assembled'. In ballet, it refers to a jump where your legs come together in the air so that you land on both feet at the same time.

Attitude A ballet position where your bent leg is lifted into the air.

Barre A rail that dancers use for support in warm-up exercises in the studio.

Battement A French word meaning 'beat'. In ballet, it refers to extending your leg either in front, to the side or behind you.

Chassé A French word meaning 'chased'. In ballet, it refers to a step where your feet slide out to the next position.

Coda The concluding section of a dance.

Core The muscles that surround the central part of the body, including the lower back, stomach and pelvis.

Crescendo An Italian word that means 'getting louder' or more intense.

Demi-pointe Dancing on the balls of your feet, a halfway point between flat feet and pointe.

Derrière A French word meaning 'behind'.

Développé A French word meaning 'developed'. In ballet, it refers to lifting and then extending your leg.

Entrée A French word that means 'entrance'. In ballet, it refers to the beginning of the dance.

Epaulement The position of your shoulders.

Fondu A French word meaning 'melted'. In ballet, it refers to smoothly bending on one leg.

Grand allegro Grand is a French word meaning 'big' and allegro is an Italian word meaning 'quick'. Together, they refer to large, expressive jumps in ballet.

Jeté A French word meaning 'thrown'. In ballet, it refers to a leap from one foot to the other.

Pas de deux A French phrase meaning 'step of two'. In ballet, it refers to two dancers performing steps together.

Passé A French word meaning 'passed'. In ballet it refers to bringing one of your feet to the side of your knee with pointed toes.

Petit allegro Petit is a French word meaning 'little' and allegro is an Italian word meaning 'quick'. Together, they refer to small, quick jumps in ballet.

Pirouette A French word meaning 'whirl'. In ballet, it describes a spin on one foot.

Plié A French word meaning 'bent'. In ballet, it refers to bending your knees.

Pointe Dancing on the very tips of your toes while wearing special pointe shoes to support your feet.

Relevé A French word meaning 'raised'. In ballet, it refers to rising onto the balls of your feet or your tiptoes.

Révérence A bow or curtsey at the end of a dance to say thank you to the teacher, musicians or audience.

Rond de jambe A French phrase that means 'round of the leg'. In ballet, it refers to moving your leg in a circular motion.

Sauté A French word meaning 'jumped'. In ballet, it refers to any kind of jump.

Sissonne A type of jump starting on two feet and landing on one foot, with the legs spread in the air.

Spotting A technique to help ballet dancers feel less dizzy where they keep their eyes fixed on one spot for as long as possible while they turn.

Temps levé A French phrase meaning 'lifted step'. In ballet, it refers to a small hop, taking off and landing on the same foot.

Tour de force An incredible or amazing accomplishment.

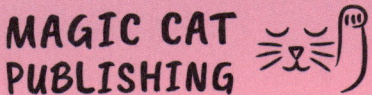
MAGIC CAT PUBLISHING

Anything Is Possible with Ballet © 2025 Lucky Cat Publishing Ltd
Text © 2025 Steven McRae
Illustrations © 2025 Margaux Carpentier
First Published in 2025 by Magic Cat Publishing, an imprint of Lucky Cat Publishing Ltd,
Unit 2 Empress Works, 24 Grove Passage, London E2 9FQ, UK
EU Authorised Representative Magic Cat Publishing, an imprint of Lucky Cat Publishing Ltd,
PAKTA svetovanje d.o.o., Stegne 33, Ljubljana, Slovenia

The right of Steven McRae to be identified as the author of this work and Margaux Carpentier to be identified as the illustrator of this work has been asserted by them in accordance with the Copyright, Designs and Patents Act, 1988 (UK).

No part of this publication may be reproduced, stored in a retrieval system, or transmitted, in any form, or by any means, electrical, mechanical, photocopying, recording or otherwise without the prior written permission of the publisher or a licence permitting restricted copying.

A catalogue record for this book is available from the British Library.

ISBN 978-1-915569-81-3

The illustrations were created digitally
Set in Blunt, Bourton and Le Havre Rounded

Published by Rachel Williams and Jenny Broom
Designed by Kim Hankinson

Manufactured in China

9 8 7 6 5 4 3 2 1